Diego the Dinosaur's Easter Surprise

Written & Illustrated by

Beth McGlynn

It was a fresh spring morning. The sun was shining on the daffodils and tulips, which Diego loved for their vibrant colours. Diego the dinosaur was doing his morning stretches and let out a big roar to let all his friends know he was awake. He was in a particularly happy mood today, as it was Easter! He didn't know exactly what Easter was, but he'd heard it was magical, and we all know how much Diego loves magical things!

Diego began his Easter filled day of fun by exploring the meadow and admiring as many flowers as he could. He saw pink ones, yellow ones, orange ones, purple ones and even white ones. He had never seen so many, it was beautiful. As he reached the end of the meadow he saw a hand-painted sign. It read, "Easter Egg Hunt This Way." Diego wondered what it was and followed the sign.

Diego followed the sign and came across some footprints. "I wonder who these belong to?" Diego thought. After following them for a while he heard giggling up ahead. Diego peeked through the bushes and saw a fluffy white bunny picking up colourful round objects. "Hello," whispered Diego, as he didn't want to scare the bunny. "Hi, my name is Buttons. What's yours?" Replied the Bunny.

"Nice to meet you, I'm Diego. What are those round things you're collecting?" Diego asked. "They're Easter eggs. I'm collecting as many as I can find in the Easter egg hunt." "Ah," Diego thought, "so this is what an Easter egg hunt is." "I've never done an Easter egg hunt before. Can you help me?"

Diego and Buttons hopped down the trail. Buttons explained to Diego that the Easter eggs came in all different sizes and colours and that they wanted to collect as many as possible because they all had different surprises inside. "What's inside the eggs?" asked Diego. "Some have chocolate, others have sweets, but one really special egg has an extra special surprise. Even I don't know what it is!" "Wow!" said Diego. "Let's find as many as we can!"

Diego followed Buttons and they picked up all kinds of colourful eggs. Diego was confused as to why they were in such strange places...in trees, under rocks...but then there was a whole tray just left by the side of the tree so he quickly put those in his basket! He was having so much fun. They continued the hunt for a bit longer when they heard a strange "baa" noise. What could that be?

The "baa" noise was getting louder and before Buttons and Diego could find any more eggs, another white fluffy animal jumped out at them. But it wasn't a bunny, it had much smaller ears. "Hi, my name is Larry the Lamb." "Nice to meet you," Buttons and Diego said as they introduced themselves.

"Have you found any special eggs yet?" Larry asked. "Not yet," said Diego, "but I did find all these ones." Larry looked confused, he'd never seen eggs like that before. They weren't as colourful as the normal ones they found. "Maybe they're the special ones, Diego," said Larry. "We'll have to wait and see!"

The three of them continued their Easter egg hunt. Diego was happy he had made two new friends and was having a wonderful day among the flowers, and he loved collecting the eggs! Just when he thought it couldn't get any better, as they went around the corner, they saw a giant lake. The sun was sparkling on the water, and there were lots of people splashing around. Diego thought this looked familiar, but just before he could remember where from, he heard…"Hi, Diego!" He turned around to see Peter Penguin. He'd been swimming in the lake! What a nice surprise!

The three of them continued along the trail and collected as many eggs as they could before they reached the finish. Buttons said they were nearly at the end. "Red one, blue one, shiny yellow one," Diego was filling his basket as quickly as he could. Then they reached the end of the trail and began to open their eggs.

They all took turns opening their eggs. Buttons started and got chocolate, which didn't last long as he soon ate it. Larry went next and got sweets, which he was very happy with but decided to save for later.

Diego went next and decided to open one of the ones he found by the side of the path, but before he could open his egg, it started to crack. The three of them watched as the crack got bigger. Larry said that he'd never seen that before.

"This must be the extra special egg," said Buttons. They all excitedly watched as the crack turned into a pop and a bright yellow tiny chick looked out. "This is really special," said Larry. Diego hadn't seen anything jump out of an egg before. "This really is magic," said Diego. The chick waddled over to Diego and pecked at his feet, he was tiny. "What's your name?" said Diego.

"I'm Charlie," said the chick. "Nice to meet you, I'm Diego." "Are you the special Easter surprise?" Diego asked. Charlie was a bit unsure "What's Easter?" he asked. They all looked at each other, confused. "Where did you find the egg?" asked Larry. Diego explained that he found a whole tray of them by the tree. Larry soon realised that the tray was full of chick eggs, not Easter eggs, but it was too late. They turned around to find the whole tray of eggs had hatched, and there were now lots of chicks.

Diego was so happy, he had never had so many friends before. There were too many to count, and they kept following him around. It was all thanks to Buttons and Larry, who had helped him on his first Easter egg hunt. It may have gone slightly differently than normal, with the help of lots of chicks, but sometimes things don't always go to plan. Diego was happy about that.

Diego was back in the flower meadow and was showing the chicks all the different colours. He watched as the sun started to set and thought about the beautiful day he had had. It was magical, full of surprises, and his best Easter ever!